Scandinavian STITCH CRAFT

Unique Projects and Patterns for Inspired Embroidery

KARIN HOLMBERG

RUNNING PRESS
PHILADELPHIA · LONDON

Books published by Running Press are available at special discounts for bulk purchases in the United States by corporations, institutions, and other organizations. For more information, please contact the Special Markets Department at the Perseus Books Group, 2300 Chestnut Street, Suite 200, Philadelphia, PA 19103, or call (800) 810-4145, ext. 5000, or e-mail special.markets@perseusbooks.com.

ISBN 978-0-7624-4854-8
Library of Congress Control Number: 2013930107

E-book ISBN 978-0-7624-4856-2

9   8   7   6   5   4   3   2   1
Digit on the right indicates the number of this printing

Designed by Corinda Cook
Edited by Eva Kruk
North America edition edited by Cindy De La Hoz
Typography: Caslon, Eurostile, Fairfield, Filosofia, Franklin Gothic, and Professor

Running Press Book Publishers
2300 Chestnut Street
Philadelphia, PA 19103-4371

Visit us on the web!
www.runningpress.com

CONTENTS

INTRODUCTION

Folk textile, folk costumes, and the rich tradition of embroidery in Sweden have long been my main sources of inspiration. Bright colors and fanciful patterns used to be combined in ways that were often highly original, fascinating, and at times a bit surprising. Not everything was grey homespun; rather, people put a lot of time and work into decorating everyday items. That says something of the human drive to be creative.

Embroidery is a way of personalizing home textiles and clothes; it is also accessible. All you really need to get started is a needle and thread and you'll be ready to embroider almost anything. Embroideries are easy to take with you: sew on the train, at the coffee shop, or with friends.

The main purpose of this book is to inspire. If you still want to make the designs exactly as seen here, you can use the patterns in the back of the book. Tracing paper tucked into the back cover of the book will help. Trace the pattern onto the paper and use it as a guide as you stitch. I have selected eight classic regional embroideries and show how they can be done traditionally or developed in new directions. My hope is that you will discover the textile treasure trove that these embroideries constitute, as well as be inspired to interpret them in your own way. Take out the needle and start to embroider!

Karin

REGIONAL STITCHES

All embroidery techniques that I use in the book originate in old Swedish folk textiles. Often it's not known precisely when a new technique came into use, or who was the first person to sew it, but most likely people were initially trying to copy exclusive woven damask fabrics. They then borrowed patterns and templates from one another, passing them back and forth between the homesteads. This is how, over time, certain embroideries became popular and distinctive to specific parts of the country.

Järvsö stitch was a way for peasant women to show off their own craft skill as well as the financial status of their farm. To display their work, every farm had one or more beds made with richly decorated bedding, intended only for show. Hanging linens and pillowcases were embroidered with red cotton floss. Some of the floss wasn't true "Turkish red" and has faded over time, so the embroideries now appear more pink. The motifs are various florals, more or less stylized. The techniques used are one-sided flat stitch and stem stitch. The Järvsö stitch is set apart by the characteristic "tassels" sewn with four or five stitches. In books this type of stitch sometimes goes by the name of "tassel stitch." Järvsö stitch is fairly fast and easy to sew. It may be wise to secure the long stitches that make up the flowers with small stitches. This will help keep the embroidery in place.

Delsbo stitch is similar to Järvsö stitch, though the patterns tend to be slightly different. The motifs are usually flowers and leaves, but they are rounder than the somewhat more sprawling forms of Järvsö stitch. Delsbo stitch is also sewn using red cotton floss and one-sided flat stitch. Here it is common to secure the stitches with a garland of stem stitches around the center of the flower. The patterns were often drawn using cutout templates made from paper or birch bark. These were passed down through the generations and shared by several embroideresses. This practice might explain why many embroideries are so similar and stylized within a particular region.

12

Anundsjö stitch is the only technique in this book associated with a specific person: Brita-Kajsa Karlsdotter. She lived in the Ångermanland region in the nineteenth century and took up embroidery late in life. This is said to explain the somewhat shaky and charming style of this type of embroidery. According to one story about her, she would always ask her children and grandchildren to thread her needles when they visited. That way she could continue embroidering on her own. Here too the motif was red flowers with thin stems and lobed leaves. They were given their distinct look by her securing the long stitch with a small, diagonal one. A recurring theme is that she would embroider her initials: BKD, the year, and the letters ÄRTHG, which is a Swedish acronym for "the credit belongs to God." Anundsjö stitch doesn't take much time to sew, and you needn't worry too much about the stitches being the same exact length; "imperfection" is part of its charm!

Halland stitch is most often seen on pillowcases. They are embroidered on just one of the short ends, as that is what can be seen from the room. The patterns differ quite a bit from other types of stitches. Halland stitch has a far more stylized and geometric type of design. It consists of circles, triangles, stars, and heart shapes; sometimes composed to form flowers and a sort of tree of life. Another distinctive trait is the laid filling stitch that fills the shapes. This is sewn by drawing up threads to form a net, either straight and along the thread or diagonally, which is secured using various types of stitches. The edges are neatly hidden using stem stitch, or chain stitch. One-sided flat stitch does occur, but it is more common to cover larger surfaces using herringbone stitch. If the stitches are too long, they can be secured using chain stitch, or stem stitch. Blue or red cotton floss is commonly used. By combining these two colors with different laid filling stiches one can create nearly infinite variations on this embroidery. Halland stitch demands a high level of accuracy, but you get into it quickly and I think it can be quite relaxing to simply fill circles with different stitches.

Blekinge stitch shares traits with many other regional stitches. It combines one-sided flat stitch, encroaching satin stitch (often using two shades of thread intertwined to create further nuance), laid filling stitch, stem stitch, and French knots. Motifs include flowers, flower baskets, birds, stylized humans, and the like. The stitch is sewn using cotton floss in various shades of blue and pink. The embroideries were usually done on wall hangings that were displayed in the house for festive occasions, in which case they might depict scenes from the Bible. If you're not that religious, Blekinge stitch is a golden opportunity to bring out your most romantic side and indulge in massive amounts of pink flowers.

Sew-on (*påsöm* in Swedish) is a satin stitch, sewn with wool floss (often called Zephyr yarn, a rather soft and fuzzy woolen yarn in bright, clear colors). This stitch exists virtually only on the folk costume from Floda in Dalarna. That is why it sometimes goes by the name Dala-Floda embroidery. The pattern consists of a cornucopia of flowers and leaves, everything from naturalistic violets to fanciful roses. Apparently, certain embroiderers in Floda embroidered completely freehand, drawing inspiration from nature around them. However, many used templates as an aid. One template always began with the largest flowers; these were placed on the bonnet, jacket, and skirt hem of the folk costume and then the space around was filled in with leaves and smaller flowers. The name comes from saying that one "sewed on" something. Several embroiderers in Floda were so skilled that they could make a living embroidering and selling their work. I try not to play favorites with embroidery techniques, but this is probably the stitch that I think is the most fun and yields the best-looking results. Unfortunately the rather thick wool yarn makes the technique suitable primarily for clothing and perhaps the occasional cushion.

Skåne wool embroidery is also sewn using wool floss on homespun or broadcloth, but is distinguished from sew-on in several ways. It is usually sewn with floss that is harder wound, creating a somewhat coarse effect. The color scheme is red, green, dark blue, white, and ochre. Religious themes are common, especially Adam and Eve in Paradise, with wonderful Naivistic people and tons of plants and fantasy creatures filling up every inch of space. In folk art one speaks of *horror vacui*, or fear of empty space. Skåne embroidery is a prime example of this. It was especially common as decoration on seat pads for carriages and cushions. This embroidery shares subject matter and palette with *röllakan* weaves. It is likely that one embroidered using scraps of yarn from the looms.

14

There are also embroideries made entirely out of geometric shapes, such as stars and diamonds, which look even more like woven tapestries. The methods used are flat stitch, stem stitch, chain stitch (used to fill larger surfaces), and twist stitch. If you're like me and love florals with tons of detail, this embroidery is a lot of fun to work with. Since chain stitch fills an area well, it doesn't take as long as you may think.

Blackwork has its origin in court costumes from the continent where it is also called Spanish stitch, or Holbein stitch (after the artist Hans Holbein the younger, who skillfully depicted it in royal portraits). In Sweden you see it mainly on scarves for folk costumes from Leksand, Åhl, and Gagnef in Dalarna. Blackwork is a combination of cross stitch, flat stitch, and back stitch, sewn with black silk on fine evenweave linen. Since you count threads when you embroider, you get very exact geometric patterns. In other words, this takes both good eyesight and the patience of a saint, but I think it's fun to do these types of big and complicated projects once in a while, for a change. You can also experiment more freely with this technique and create very modern, graphic embroideries.

PROJECTS

Refer to the resource guides beginning on page 84 for Karin Holmberg's invaluable information on techniques, tools, and lessons that will help even the most inexperienced crafter get started on the following projects.

TOWEL: DECK OF CARDS

The geometric patterns of Halland stitch inspired me to make a kitchen towel with a deck of cards theme. Use it as a baking cloth and play solitaire while you wait for your bread to rise!

TECHNIQUE: *Halland* stitch
SUPPLIES:
- red and black linen floss 16/2
- white sheeting, approximately 49 x 64 cm/ 19.2" x 25.2", or a readymade white cotton kitchen towel, approximately 45 x 60 cm/ 17.7" x 23.6"
- cotton tape for hanging

PATTERN: see page 99

METHOD: Fold in all edges and hem the fabric by hand or machine (or use a readymade towel). Transfer the pattern and embroider using Halland stitch. The cards should have different laid filling stitches and back stitch around the edges.

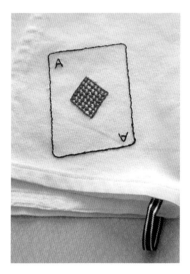

TOWEL: DELSBO FLOWER

The actual embroidery doesn't always have to be big to make an impact. In this case one lone little Delsbo flower is used to decorate the towel.

TECHNIQUE: *Delsbo* stitch
SUPPLIES:

- red pearl floss, or DMC mouliné
- white linen cloth, approximately 49 x 64 cm/ 19.2" x 25.2", or a readymade white linen kitchen towel, approximately 45 x 60 cm/ 17.7" x 23.6"
- cotton tape for hanging
- optional lace tape

PATTERN: See page 98

METHOD: Fold in all edges and hem the fabric by hand or machine (skip this step if you're using a readymade towel). Sew on the lace tape, if using. Sew on the cotton tape for hanging.

Mark the center of the towel. Transfer the pattern and embroider one-sided flat stitch and stem stitch. Use one thread pearl floss, or three threads mouliné floss. Secure all ends and iron the towel smooth.

TOWEL: WHITE BINE

Järvsö stitch is usually sewn with red floss on white fabric, but that doesn't mean it has to be that way. You can achieve interesting effects simply by inverting the colors! This towel also happens to be sewn using cotton floss that isn't originally meant for embroidery. This gives a somewhat more sprawling look than usual.

TECHNIQUE: *Järvsö* stitch
SUPPLIES:

- white cotton floss 8/2
- red sheeting, approximately 49 x 64 cm/ 19.2" x 25.2", or a readymade red cotton kitchen towel, approximately 45 x 60 cm/ 17.7" x 23.6"

PATTERN: see page 98

METHOD: Fold in all raw edges and hem the fabric by hand or machine (or use a readymade towel). Draw up the wave-shaped bine on the towel. Transfer *Järvsö* flowers from the pattern pages and place them where you see fit. Draw little stems here and there. Embroider with one-sided flat stitch and fill in with tassel stitch to create leaves on the stems.

APRON: KITCHEN GARDEN

If you're lucky enough to find a pretty apron at a flea market or in your grandmother's attic, and it happens to be completely unadorned, you can let loose with needle and thread and make it your own. The circles are drawn using glasses, cups, or tea candles, depending on what size you'd like the resulting embroidery to be.

TECHNIQUE: *Halland* stitch
SUPPLIES:

- a white cotton apron
- red and blue DMC embroidery floss

PATTERN: see page 100

METHOD: Draw circles, hearts, and any similar shapes you like, using a pencil or marker pen. Attach the hoop and be careful to stretch the fabric properly and evenly. Sew laid filling stitches using two threads in one or two colors. I encourage you to vary things, use different stitches on the apron and around the edges. Embroider as much or as little as you see fit.

POTHOLDERS: ROSES AND TULIPS

Sewing your own potholders takes some doing, but it's a whole lot of fun! Here the embroidery serves the same purpose as when you quilt a patchwork blanket. The result is a flexible yet heat-resistant potholder.

TECHNIQUE: running stitch, inspired by *Delsbo* and *Järvsö* patterns

SUPPLIES:

- cotton fabric, two pieces of 18 x 18 cm/ 7" x 7" each (you may want to use a patterned fabric for the back, as the embroidery won't look as nice there)
- wadding, 16 x 16 cm/ 6.3" x 6.3"
- tape for the hanger
- DMC mouliné in colors that go with the fabric

PATTERN: see page 101

METHOD: Draw the pattern you want to embroider on the monochrome piece of fabric. Fold the fabric around the wadding, leaving 1 cm/ 0.4" seam allowance around the edge. Place the fabric on the back of the potholder. Cut a piece of the tape, making sure it's long enough to use as hanger. Place it in one corner, between the fabric and the wadding and pin closely around the entire potholder. Make sure the corners are nice and straight. Sew it shut with close running stitch, or using a sewing machine.

When the potholder is finished, it's time to embroider it. Pin together all three layers in a few places, so that the wadding doesn't bunch as you sew. Sew running stitch, through all three layers, along the edges of the pattern using two threads of mouliné floss. Don't pull too hard; if you do, the potholder will end up bubbly and crooked. Secure the floss on the back by making a few small stitches around each other. Thread the needle into only the upper layer of fabric and pull it up a little further away. Cut the floss close to the fabric.

Please note: If you would like lace around the edges, as on the red potholder, it is a good idea to first sew it onto one piece of fabric, before sewing the actual potholder together. Otherwise you will end up with a whole lot of pins.

TEA COZY: BLEKINGE FLOWERS

If you think tea should be brewed in a pot and kept warm all through Sunday breakfast, a tea cozy is a good sewing and embroidery project. You can make the embroidery small, or decorate the entire cozy using needle and thread.

TECHNIQUE: *Blekinge* stitch

SUPPLIES:

- linen outer fabric, 2 pieces of 26 x 26 cm/ 10.2" x 10.2" each and 1 piece of 8 x 70 cm/ 3" x 27.6"
- cotton fabric for the lining, 2 pieces of 26 x 26 cm/ 10.2" x 10.2" and 1 piece of 8 x 70 cm/ 3" x 27.6"
- wadding for the lining, 2 pieces of 26 x 26 cm/ 10.2" x 10.2" each, and 1 piece of 8 x 70 cm/ 3" x 27.6"
- bias strip, approximately 75 cm/ 29.5"
- DMC mouliné, in pink, blue, yellow, white

PATTERN: see page 102

METHOD: The outer fabric, the lining, and the wadding are supposed to make two side panels and one strip for the middle. Cut the same rounding on two adjacent corners on all side panels. Use a sewing machine to zigzag the raw edges of all pieces of outer fabric and lining.

Draw the pattern you'd like to embroider on the outer fabric, perhaps in the center of one of the side panels. Embroider Blekinge stitch using two threads mouliné floss. Use a hoop so that the fabric doesn't bunch.

When you've finished the embroidery, iron the fabric from the back on the highest setting.

Assemble the tea cozy as follows: Begin by sewing the outer part and the handle.

Cut 8 cm/ 3.1" of the bias strip, fold it lengthwise, and sew two straight seams about 1 mm/ 0.04" from the edge. Place the strip crosswise in the middle of the face of the centerpiece and pin it down. Pin the centerpiece to one of the side panels, face to face, and sew together the parts using a straight seam, 1 cm/ 0.4" from the edge.

Pin together the other side of the centerpiece to the other side panel and sew them together the same way as the first. Press the seams apart from the reverse side using a hot iron.

Turn the cozy inside out, so that the face is outward and sew a reinforcing straight seam 1 mm/ 0.04" on either side of each seam. The outside is now finished. The bias strip at the top is like a handle for the tea cozy.

Sew the lining. Place the wadding on each one of the parts of the fabric used for lining and sew it in place using a few lengthwise straight seams. Sew together the components of the lining the same way you did the outside. Cut away any loose threads or wadding poking out.

Insert the lining into the outer shell, so that you have a nearly finished tea cozy.

Pin together the lining and the outer shell along the bottom and sew both pieces together, using a straight seam about 0.5 cm/ 0.2" from the edge. Even out the edge using scissors.

Fold the remaining piece of bias strip around the bottom edge and attach using a straight seam, as close to the edge of the strip as possible. Make sure that the seam attaches to the tape on the inside as well as on the outside of the tea cozy.

PLACEMATS: BLEKINGE FLOWERS

It's nice to match the tea cozy with placemats made using the same technique. Try to position the embroideries so that they work with plates and silverware.

TECHNIQUE: *Blekinge* stitch
SUPPLIES:

- linen fabric, 2 pieces of 35 x 48 cm/ 13.8" x 19"
- DMC mouliné in pink, blue, yellow, and white

PATTERN: see page 102

METHOD: Zigzag all raw edges of fabric. Draw the pattern using a marker pen, or a pencil. It's a good idea to draw the stems all the way out to the edge, even though you'll be folding in the seam allowance later. Embroider Blekinge stitch using two threads mouliné floss. Use a hoop for best results.

Fold in the hems 1 cm/ 0.4" all around, then another 1 cm/ 0.4", so that the zigzag seam doesn't show. The placemat should now measure 31 x 44 cm/ 12.2" x 17.3". Pin and sew a straight seam using the machine, or hem by hand. Iron the finished placemat on the highest setting.

HOODIE: DALA BOY

If you don't have the time or patience to embroider the whole jacket, you can sew a flower here and there and still achieve a gorgeous effect. The back, the front, and the hood are easy to embroider and you can use a hoop in all those places.

TECHNIQUE: "sew-on"
SUPPLIES:
- wool floss, Tuna wool yarn, or the equivalent, in various colors
- a monochrome cotton tricot hoodie

PATTERN: see pages 103–104

METHOD: Transfer the patterns to cardboard or thick paper, and cut out the templates. Place them wherever you see fit on the hoodie. It's easiest to do this when somebody is wearing it, so that you can really see how the patterns fit on the body. Draw around the edges using a marker pen. Start with the largest flowers, then fill in smaller ones as well as leaves and stems. Embroider "sew-on." Use a hoop wherever possible. Be careful not to pull the stitches too tight, especially on the sleeves. Wash the finished hoodie, either by hand or using the wool cycle. Dry flat.

HOODIE: DALA MAIDEN

The lavish floral embroideries on the jackets of the folk costumes from Floda, Dalarna, are inspiring. Not many people use folk costumes these days, as we tend toward easy-to-wear tricot clothing. Why not combine the two styles?

This is a rather large project that takes its sweet time. You'll need skill, as well as patience, to get the embroideries on the sleeves right, since you're not sewing on flat fabric.

TECHNIQUE: "sew-on"
SUPPLIES:
- wool floss, Swedish "Tuna" wool yarn, or the equivalent, in various colors
- a monochrome cotton tricot hoodie

PATTERN: see pages 103–104

METHOD: Follow the instructions for the "Dala boy" hoodie. Once the pattern has been placed on the back it's easy to draw, as long as the hoodie is on a flat surface. It's still a good idea to try the hoodie on before you start to embroider. That way you can make sure that the pattern ends up where you intended.

LEGGINGS: PARADISE

Personalize your favorite leggings with winding Järvsö stitch vines. Here they're sewn in fine pink silk, but mouliné floss would work equally well.

TECHNIQUE: *Järvsö* stitch
SUPPLIES:

- silk floss, or DMC mouliné in one or more shades of pink or red
- a pair of leggings

PATTERN: see page 105

METHOD: Draw up the pattern on the legs using a marker pen. Embroider Järvsö stitch using two threads. You may want to use a smaller hoop for the flowers. The stems can be sewn without one, but make sure not to tighten the stitches too much—the leggings need to retain their stretchiness.

T-SHIRT: THE OTHER SIDE OF LEKSAND

Blackwork, a fine and precise technique, is traditionally used on the shawl that goes with the Leksand folk costume. Here it's interpreted more freely and placed on the side of a T-shirt, though the stitch and colors remain the same.

TECHNIQUE: free blackwork
SUPPLIES:
- black DMC mouliné
- a T-shirt in a suitable size
- evenweave linen, or Aida

PATTERN: see page 106

METHOD: Mark the area of the T-shirt that you want to embroider. The best way is to baste a thread along the contours; you can pull it out later. That way you will avoid leaving traces of a marker pen. It's a good idea to have someone else wear the T-shirt so that you can see what the pattern really looks like on the body. Then cut out a piece of linen, or Aida in the size of the pattern. Sew whipstitch around the edge so that it doesn't fray. Then baste the supporting fabric inside the marking. Embroider blackwork with two or three threads mouliné floss, through both the linen and the T-shirt. You may want to sketch shapes onto the linen that you can fill in when you embroider, or you could sew completely freehand. Keep in mind that the empty spaces between embroideries also form pretty patterns. Make sure to bring the needle through between the threads in the linen weave, or it will be hard to take it out. When you're done sewing, it's time to take the supporting linen out. Cut the weave with embroidery scissors around the edges of the finished embroidery, to get rid of the hemmed edges. Now carefully pull the loose threads out. Take one at a time, first horizontally, then vertically. The actual embroidery now remains on the T-shirt, aligned and even.

T-SHIRT: PORCELAIN FLOWERS

This is the freest take on a regional stitch in this book. The question is if you can even call this blackwork, as it is sewn using white floss.

TECHNIQUE: free blackwork
SUPPLIES:
- DMC white mouliné
- a T-shirt in a suitable size
- evenweave linen, or Aida

PATTERN: see page 107

METHOD: Draw the pattern using a white marker pen, but don't push too hard because the fabric breaks through a fair amount with this pattern, and you don't want to see traces of the pen through the embroidery.

Next, cut pieces of evenweave linen, or Aida, to cover the shape of the pattern, in this case approximately 5 x 5 cm/ 2" x 2". Sew whipstitch around all edges to prevent the weave from fraying. Pin and baste the weave over the pattern so that it ends up right on top. Now draw the shapes again, on the weave. Embroider through both the weave and the T-shirt with two threads mouliné floss. Fill the shape you've drawn with cross stitch and/or flat stitch. Make sure that you bring the needle through between the threads in the supporting weave, or you will have a hard time removing it. To remove the hemmed edge, use embroidery scissors to cut the weave around the embroidery. Carefully pull the threads that are now loose. Remove one at a time, first horizontally, then vertically. The actual embroidery now remains on the T-shirt, aligned and neat. Continue with the rest of the patterns and shapes. The stem that ties the flowers together is sewn using back stitch and doesn't need supporting weave.

Please note: If you're not the pedantic type you can embroider cross stitch, flat stitch, and back stitch freehand, but the T-shirt will end up with a more "unique" look.

T-SHIRT: BOUQUET

Blekinge stitch, with its pastel palette and cute subject matter, is very well suited to children's clothes. This particular pattern, with a little flower basket in laid filling stitch, is one you often see on old wall hangings and cushions done in this technique.

TECHNIQUE: *Blekinge* stitch
SUPPLIES:
- cotton floss, DMC embroidery floss, or DMC mouliné, in blue, pink, yellow, turquoise
- a white T-shirt in a suitable color

PATTERN: see page 104

METHOD: Draw the pattern on the center front of the T-shirt. Attach the hoop and embroider Blekinge stitch using two threads. Mixing threads in two different colors is a great way to create variation here. Lightly iron the T-shirt to get rid of the indentation from the hoop.

SWEATPANTS: LITTLE TUSSOCK

These sweatpants for kids are embroidered using the softest tapestry wool, to prevent itchiness on the legs. The pattern is placed at the bottom of the leg, where it's relatively easy to sew and won't wear out too fast.

TECHNIQUE: "sew-on"
SUPPLIES:
- DMC tapestry wool in various colors
- one pair kid-size black sweatpants

PATTERN: see page 104

METHOD: Draw the pattern using a white marker pen. Use a hoop if you can fit it in;

if not, try keeping the fabric as flat as possible using one hand. Be careful not to pull the stitches too tight. The wool can be split into one or two threads, if you like. Experiment to figure out how thick you want the embroidery to be.

T-SHIRT: SWEETHEART

Halland stitch is usually done using blue and red floss on white fabric. Here I've changed things around a bit. In other words, you can get ketchup all over this and it won't be a big deal!

TECHNIQUE: *Halland* stitch
SUPPLIES:
- DMC mouliné, white and blue
- a red T-shirt in a suitable size

PATTERN: see page 109

METHOD: Trace the heart-shaped template and place it on the T-shirt. Draw around the template using a marker pen or pencil. Draw several hearts next to it, but make sure to leave enough space for the edge stitches. Attach a small hoop around one heart at a time and embroider laid filling stitch inside the shapes. Sew using two threads. Finish with an edging of back stitch, chain stitch, and/or running stitch. Continue with the rest of the hearts.

Please note: It's easier to embroider T-shirts that aren't too ribbed. For this reason, try to find tricot shirts that are as smooth and sturdy as possible.

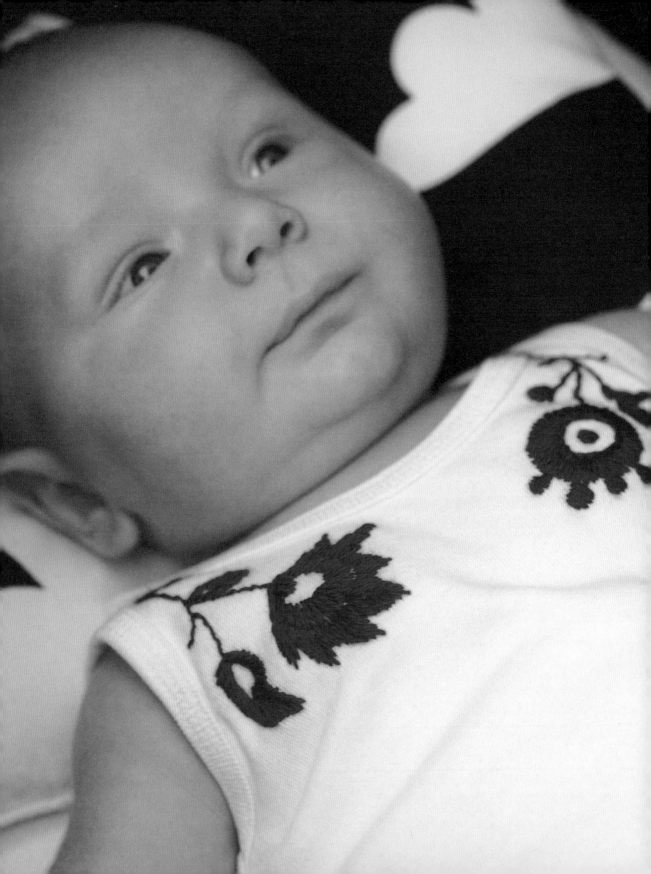

ONESIE: MARIGOLD

Sure, baby will grow out of this piece of clothing pretty fast, but for the short time it fits it will look like a miracle in bloom. This onesie looks extra pretty with the matching hat.

TECHNIQUE: *Delsbo* stitch
SUPPLIES:

- red cotton floss, DMC embroidery floss
- a white onesie, baby-sized

PATTERN: see page 110

METHOD: Draw the pattern with a marker pen, if you like you can let it go all the way around the neck, or only the front. Embroider Delsbo stitch using two threads cotton floss. Be extra careful and use a light hand, since it is difficult to fit a hoop into this small area. The tricot in onesies is often ribbed, which makes it extra elastic. Take care that the stitches don't bunch too much.

BABY HAT: MARIGOLD

TECHNIQUE: *Delsbo* stitch
SUPPLIES:

- red cotton floss, DMC embroidery floss
- a white, baby-sized hat

PATTERN: see page 110

METHOD: Follow the instructions for the onesie. Place the pattern where you see fit: to one side, on both sides, or maybe on the back.

PANTIES: CANDY

These might not be everyday wear, but there's something luxurious about spending time and effort on decorating regular cotton panties. Go ahead and mix colors and patterns, embroider big, or just a small monogram.

TECHNIQUE: freely interpreted *Delsbo* stitch
SUPPLIES:

- DMC embroidery floss, or pearl floss, in various colors
- cotton panties in your size

PATTERN: see page 111

METHOD: Follow the instructions for the lingerie set "Delsbo rose" on the next spread, but experiment freely with different colors and compositions.

LINGERIE SET: DELSBO ROSE

A lot of lingerie is decorated with embroideries and the most exclusive is hand-embroidered by you!

TECHNIQUE: *Delsbo* stitch
SUPPLIES:

- red cotton floss, DMC embroidery floss
- a white bra and a pair of white panties

PATTERN: see page 111

METHOD: Draw the pattern on the underwear where you'd like it to be. Keep wear and tear in mind. For instance, embroideries will wear faster if they're placed right on your behind. Don't think too much though; function should follow form in this instance.

Embroider Delsbo stitch. Use a hoop if it fits. Remember not to tighten the stitches too much, as the fabric still needs to stretch.

SOCKS: MISS FRÄKEN

Do you get confused in the laundry room and wonder which socks go together? Mark them with matching embroideries!

TECHNIQUE: *Järvsö* stitch
SUPPLIES:

- DMC mouliné in one or more shades of pink or red
- a pair of socks

PATTERN: see page 112

METHOD: Put the socks on. Draw the pattern with a white marker pen. Embroider Järvsö stitch using two threads mouliné floss. It's a good idea to keep to just the contours of the flowers. Use back stitch, which is a fairly elastic stitch. Be careful not to tighten the stitches too much! Socks need to stretch. If you think there's too much space between stitches, you can thread an extra thread through them, the same way you would using *Anundsjö* stitch (see page 95). Secure all ends and do the same on the other sock.

CUFFS: FOLKLORIC

These cuffs won't take more than a few evenings to make. They're embroidered using back stitch, rather than flat stitch, as that fits stretchy fabric well. This gives a slightly different look that still goes well with the Delsbo patterns.

TECHNIQUE: variation on *Delsbo* stitch
SUPPLIES:

- red DMC mouliné, or pearl floss
- tricot fabric, 2 pieces of 17 x 21 cm/ 6.7" x 8.3", *or* cut the bottom part off an old pair of leggings (then you'll also get a readymade hem)

PATTERN: see page 113

METHOD: Lay the fabric on a smooth surface and draw the pattern using a white marker pen. Embroider back stitch along the contours, using one thread red pearl floss, or three threads mouliné. Use the same pattern for both cuffs, or sew two completely different ones, according to your own taste.

When the embroidery is finished, fold the cuff double, face to face, and sew it together using back stitch. If you have a sewing machine that can do tricot stitch, or overlock stitch, you can obviously use it here.

CUSHION: SEWN BY ME

Brita-Kajsa, who created the *Anundsjö* stitch, often included letters in her designs. Personalize your embroidery by using initials, names, or a bit of text. The cushion will look best if the cover fits snugly. That is why I make sure the finished cover ends up a few centimeters smaller than the actual cushion.

TECHNIQUE: *Anundsjö* stitch
SUPPLIES:

- red DMC mouliné
- white linen fabric, three pieces: 40 x 40 cm/ 15.7" x 15.7" (for the front of the cover), 40 x 31 cm/ 15.7" x 12.2" and 40 x 21 cm/ 15.7" x 8.3" (for the back of the cover)
- one cushion, 40 x 40 cm/ 15.7" x 15.7"

PATTERN: see page 114

METHOD: Zigzag all raw edges on the pieces of fabric. Hem one long side on each of the two components of the back by folding the edge double so that the zigzag seam is hidden. Pin and sew, using a sewing machine.

Draw the pattern in the center of the front piece and embroider Anundsjö stitch using two threads mouliné floss. The text is sewn using back stitch. Use a hoop. Stretch or iron the finished embroidery so that it is smooth.

Arrange the front piece so that you have the face toward you. Place the shorter piece of fabric for the back over it, so that they are face to face. Last, place the longer piece of fabric for the back over that, so that it overlaps with the first. Pin all the way around and sew together using a sewing machine. Turn everything inside out so that the face is outward and stuff with a cushion that fits.

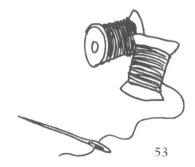

CUSHION: LUSHLY

You may want to try sewing a specific regional stitch using another type of floss than what is traditionally used. This cushion has patterns from woolen folk costume jackets, but is sewn using shiny mouliné floss that gives the impression of Asian silk embroidery instead.

TECHNIQUE: "sew-on"
SUPPLIES:

- DMC mouliné in various colors
- cotton fabric in any color you like, 2 pieces of 40 x 42 cm/ 15.7" x 16.5" each
- ribbon to tie the cover shut
- 1 inner cushion 40 x 40 cm/ 15.7" x 15.7"

PATTERN: see pages 103–104

METHOD: Zigzag around all raw edges of fabric. Hem one side of each piece by folding it double, so that the cover for the finished cushion ends up measuring 40 x 40 cm/ 15.7" x 15.7".

Draw the pattern on one of the pieces of fabric. Make sure that the hem ends up on the top edge. Embroider "sew-on" using two threads mouliné floss. Iron or stretch the finished embroidery so that it is smooth.

Place the two pieces of fabric face to face, hems facing up. Pin and sew the three remaining sides shut. Turn so that the outside faces out. Sew two or three ribbons on to each side so that you can tie the cover shut.

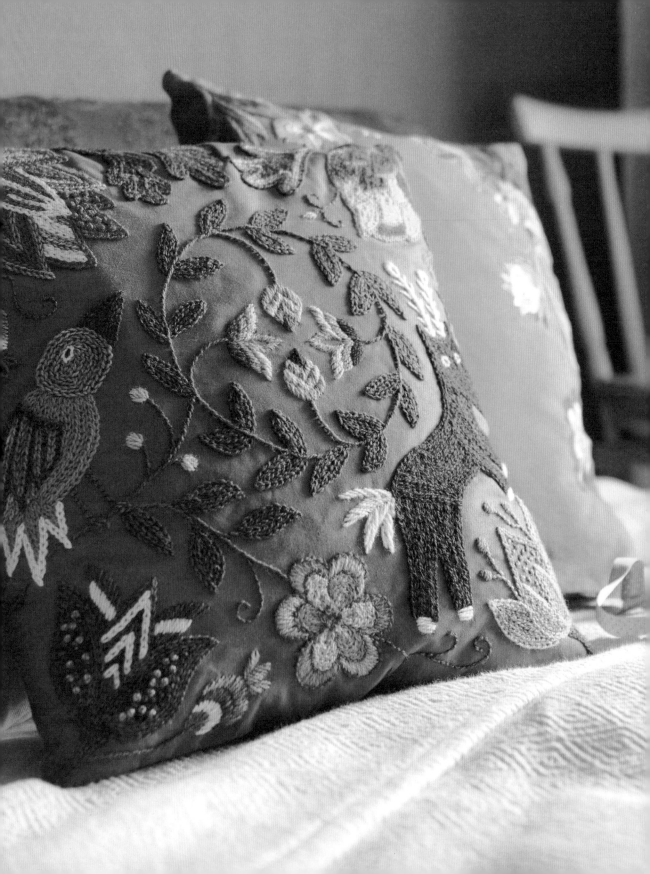

CUSHION: ÖSTERLEN GARDEN

Wool embroidery from Skåne is traditionally done on wool cloth, or so-called broadcloth, but that is expensive and hard to find. You can still achieve good results by using wool floss on cotton fabric. It's a good idea to pick a sturdier fabric here, especially if you are using thick wool floss. The embroidery will tighten up more than when you use cotton floss, but if you stretch it properly afterward it will still end up smooth. So don't panic!

TECHNIQUE: **Skåne wool embroidery**
SUPPLIES:

- **wool floss, Tuna wool yarn, or similar, in various colors**
- **dark blue cotton fabric, 3 pieces: 40 x 40 cm/ 15.7" x 15.7" (for the front of the cushion) 40 x 31 cm/ 15.7" x 12.2" and 40 x 21 cm/ 15.7" x 8.3" (for the back of the cushion)**

PATTERN: **See page 115**

METHOD: Zigzag around all raw edges. Hem one of the long sides on each piece of fabric for the back of the cushion by folding the edge double, so that the zigzag stitch isn't visible. Pin and sew by machine.

Draw the pattern using a white marker pen. Fill in the shapes using cross stitch, flat stitch, stem stitch, back stitch, and knots.

Stretch the finished embroidery on a wood panel according to instructions on page 91. Let dry and then carefully take it off.

Place the front of the cushion so that the face is toward you. Place the shorter piece of fabric for the back so that they are face to face. Finally, place the longer piece of fabric for the back on the others, so that they overlap. Pin around all of it and sew it together using a sewing machine. Turn it all so that the outside faces out.

Please note: All cushion covers can obviously be closed using a zipper if you prefer, but I find it hard to sew on zippers without causing bumps. These two methods (overlap, or ribbons to tie it shut) are easy, don't require a specific presser, and the ribbon option especially will make the pillow look extra fancy.

TABLECLOTH: BLACKWORK MODERN

The geometrical shapes of blackwork are perfect for creating more modern patterns. Take details from traditional pattern templates, change the scale and shapes, and you have an embroidery that is far more contemporary than folk costume in look and feel.

TECHNIQUE: blackwork
SUPPLIES:

- black DMC mouliné
- evenweave linen 10 threads per cm/ 28 count, 34 x 74 cm/ 13.4" x 29.1", dimensions when finished: 30 x 70 cm/ 11.8" x 27.6"

PATTERN: see page 116

METHOD: Whipstitch, or zigzag, all raw edges so that the fabric doesn't fray. Measure out the center and embroider filled and semi-filled squares using the pattern on page 116 as a guide (and the picture below) with two threads mouliné floss. Sew the squares by counting threads. One cross stitch is sewn over two threads in the weave. Once you've embroidered all the squares, draw lines for the edges using pencil, or a marker pen. Embroider these using back stitch. Fold the edge double all around and hem the tablecloth. When finished, the cloth should measure approximately 30 x 70 cm/ 11.8" x 27.6". Iron the cloth smooth.

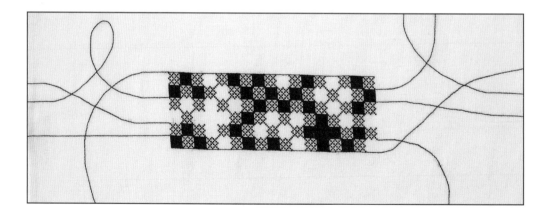

TABLECLOTH: PINK GARLAND

It's fun to study traditional embroideries and use them as inspiration to create your own patterns. This cloth borrows the floral from Järvsö stitch, while the leaves and dots are my own invention.

TECHNIQUE: Järvsö stitch, one-sided flat stitch
SUPPLIES:

- pink cotton floss, DMC embroidery floss
- linen or cotton cloth, 38 x 38 cm/ 15" x 15"

PATTERN: see page 116

METHOD: Zigzag around all edges. Measure out the center and draw the pattern around it. Embroider one-sided flat stitch and stem stitch using two threads. Hem the finished cloth by folding the edge double, pin and sew straight stitch using the sewing machine. When finished, the cloth should measure 33 x 53 cm/ 13.4" x 13.4". Iron it smooth.

TABLECLOTH: BLACKWORK TRADITIONAL

Blackwork was traditionally done using black silk floss. If you don't feel like spending a fortune on your cloth, black mouliné floss will work just as well. Sew using one or two threads to achieve different effects.

TECHNIQUE: blackwork
SUPPLIES:

- black DMC mouliné
- evenweave linen 14 threads per cm/ 36 count, 37 x 57 cm/ 14.6" x 22.4"

PATTERN: see page 117

METHOD: Whipstitch, or zigzag, all raw edges to prevent fraying. Measure the center and embroider according to the pattern using one or two threads mouliné floss. Create the squares by counting threads as you sew, one stitch is sewn over three threads in the center patterns and over four threads around the border.

Fold the edge double and hem the cloth. When finished, the cloth should measure 33 x 53 cm/ 12.9" x 20.9". If you want to hemstitch the edge, see page 97. Finish by ironing the cloth smooth.

PILLOWCASE: YOU CAN HAVE IT ALL

This pillowcase has a smooth flounce around the edge, perfect for covering with embroideries. I use text in this Anundsjö pattern too—at the very least you can dream of having it all. Look at the picture to get a more comprehensive idea of the pattern on the pillow.

TECHNIQUE: *Anundsjö* stitch
SUPPLIES:
- red DMC mouliné
- a white pillow case with a flat flounce

PATTERN: see page 118

METHOD: Draw the pattern around the entire pillow. If you would like to include text, save some space for writing it. Embroider the Anundsjö stitch using two threads mouliné floss. Iron the pillowcase smooth.

PILLOWCASE: TWO HEARTS

One of the most common uses for Halland stitch was pillowcases. The embroidery was placed on one side, the side that was turned to face the room. An added bonus is that you don't wear the floss out when it's limited to the edge of the pillow. It was common for the embroiderer to sign with the year and her maiden name. In my case that is Karin Rogersdotter.

TECHNIQUE: *Halland* stitch
SUPPLIES:

- red and blue DMC mouliné floss
- a white pillowcase

PATTERN: see page 118

METHOD: Draw the pattern on one side of the pillowcase. Embroider Halland stitch using two or three threads mouliné floss, depending on the amount of coverage you'd like. Use a hoop, especially for the laid filling stitch. You may want to iron the pillowcase to get rid of the marks from the hoop.

LAMPSHADE: LINNEA

Putting new fabric on a lampshade is easier than you might think. It will also look much nicer than the readymade shades you can buy at the store. This one is sewn using a pale pink shade on colored linen, creating a more romantic effect than that of the traditional *Anundsjö* embroidery.

TECHNIQUE: *Anundsjö* stitch
SUPPLIES:
- DMC mouliné in the color of your choice
- enough linen or cotton fabric for the lampshade
- a frame for the lampshade
PATTERN: see page 119

METHOD: Using the frame, measure the size of fabric needed. Adjust the pattern accordingly. Draw and embroider Anundsjö stitch using two threads mouliné floss. Iron the fabric smooth. Next, fold the strip of fabric face to face, and sew it together to form a tube. Turn it again so that the face is outward. Fit it over the frame. Fold in the seam allowance and sew it down using small running stitch. First sew the bottom edge, stretch the fabric properly, and pin and sew the top edge.

WALL HANGING: TURTLE DOVES

Blekinge stitch often includes cute birds flying about among romantic florals. In my opinion it can get a bit too sugary sweet, so I've given these birds a bit more weight.

TECHNIQUE: *Blekinge* stitch
SUPPLIES:

- cotton floss in a few shades of pink and blue, DMC embroidery floss
- linen, or cotton fabric, approximately 32 x 40 cm/ 12.6" x 15.7"
- a frame for mounting

PATTERN: See page 119

METHOD: Zigzag around the edges of the fabric. Draw the pattern in the center. Embroider using Blekinge stitch and two threads cotton floss. Try mixing different color threads to enhance the effect. Use a hoop. Stretch or iron the finished embroidery. Mount in the frame.

PINCUSHION: TREE

A pincushion is an absolute must for any embroiderer. It keeps your needles and pins in order and saves you from getting pricked. This one is stuffed with flaxseed, so it sits solidly on the table.

TECHNIQUE: wool embroidery with chain stitch, flat stitch, French knots, and back stitch

SUPPLIES:

- wool floss, Mora floss, or equivalent, in various colors
- broadcloth, or other sturdy wool fabric, 2 pieces of 16 x 16 cm/ 6.3" x 6.3" each
- thin cotton fabric, 2 pieces of 16 x 16 cm/ 6.3" x 6.3" each
- flaxseed for stuffing

PATTERN: see page 120

METHOD: Cut two pieces of broadcloth to measure 16 x 16 cm/ 6.3" x 6.3". In addition, cut two pieces of cotton fabric that are a few millimeters smaller. Sew them together using a sewing machine to form an inner cushion. Reserve a small hole to pour the flaxseed into. Turn it so that the outside faces out. Don't fill the inner cushion too much. Measure it so that you can still cover it with the wool fabric, leaving 1 cm/ 0.4" seam allowance. Sew the opening shut by hand.

Sketch the pattern on the broadcloth using a white marker pen. Embroider using wool floss in various colors and thicknesses, but don't use floss that's too thick because the pattern is rather small.

Now place the pieces of broadcloth face to face. Pin them together and sew using a sewing machine, but leave a larger opening than you did for the inner cushion. Insert the inner cushion into the wool cover. Fold the seam allowance, pin and sew together with small, close stitches.

SATCHEL: PEONY

This little bag was a gift from a friend. She thought I should have it. Perhaps she knew that I'd make something out of the simple, red hemp bag? In any case it wasn't long until it was covered in flowers.

TECHNIQUE: "sew-on"
SUPPLIES:

- wool floss, Tuna wool yarn, or equivalent, in various colors
- a satchel in linen, hemp, or other fabric

PATTERN: see pages 103–104

METHOD: Transfer the patterns to cardboard or sturdy paper and cut out templates. Place them on the bag and draw along the edges using a marker pen, or a pencil. Embroider "sew-on," start with the larger flowers and fill in stems and leaves in between. Be sure to secure all ends well.

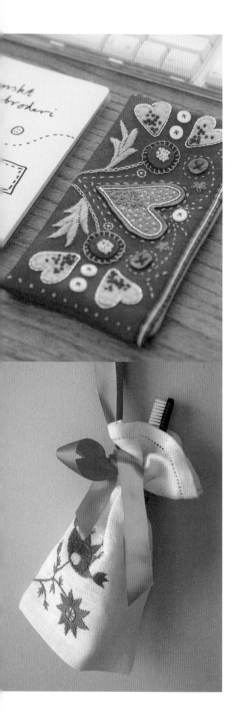

PENCIL CASE: LOVE

Transport your pencils and erasers in a sturdy case made out of colored broadcloth. Or use it for scissors, measuring tape, and the floss you're embroidering with at the moment—perfect if you're embroidering on the go!

TECHNIQUE: *Skåne* wool embroidery and appliqué
SUPPLIES:

- homespun, broadcloth, or other sturdy wool fabric, approximately 22 x 22 cm/ 8.7" x 8.7"
- craft felt, wool floss, silver floss, buttons
- zipper
- tape if desired

PATTERN: see page 121

METHOD: Fold the fabric down the middle. Cut out pieces of broadcloth, or craft felt (the latter is somewhat thinner and easier to sew through), in shapes such as hearts, circles, and the like. Arrange the shapes the way you like on the front. Pin the pieces of felt and sew them down using running stitch, knots, or whatever strikes your fancy. Sew on buttons and attach the silver floss using couching.

When the embroidery is finished, fold the fabric face to face and sew the sides together. Pin the zipper to it and then sew, using back stitch, approximately 0.5 cm/ 0.2" from the edge. If you like, you can hide this seam using tape. It's a bit fussy, but it will look great!

If you're feeling ambitious obviously you'll go ahead and embroider the back too.

SMALL BAG: PINK CARNATIONS

There's no such thing as having too many small bags for jewelry, bobby pins, or other small items. This bag has a hemstitched border and a satin ribbon to tie it shut, but you can choose whichever details you prefer.

TECHNIQUE: *Järvsö* stitch
SUPPLIES:

- pink cotton floss, DMC embroidery floss
- white linen fabric, 16 x 48 cm/ 6.3" x 18.9"
- satin ribbon, approximately 42 cm/ 16.5" long

PATTERN: see page 121

METHOD: Zigzag around all edges. Fold the fabric double. Draw the pattern using pencil or marker pen, so that it ends up just above the fold. Draw so that the stem goes all the way out to the edge of the fabric. Embroider Järvsö stitch using two threads cotton floss.

Next, make a 1 cm/ 0.4" fold on each short side, twice, so that the zigzag stitch is hidden and you get a 1 cm/ 0.4" wide hem. Pin. Sew hemstitch accordingly: Carefully cut 3–4 threads in the fabric, parallel to the hem and right under it. Pull the threads out. Make a few small stitches using sewing thread at one end of the hem. Wind the thread once or twice around 3 threads in the fabric. Make a new stitch in the hem. Do this all the way around. The threads in the fabric will bunch and create small holes. Do the same along the other edge. (See also page 97.)

Now fold the fabric face to face and pin along the long sides. Fold the ribbon double and pin it to one side, about 4 cm/ 1.6" from the top edge. Sew the pieces for the bag together on a sewing machine, or by hand using back stitch. Turn the right side out and tie the ribbon.

Please note: To prevent the satin ribbon from fraying, you can carefully burn the end. The fabric will melt and form a thin edge. This *will not* work on cotton and linen ribbons; it only works with synthetics.

PURSE: NISHIN

Skåne wool embroidery often depicts various types of animals, such as horses, deer, and lions. The blue-green wool floss seemed more maritime to me, so the motif here is fish, with a bit of inspiration from Japanese woodblock prints. *Nishin* is the Japanese word for herring.

TECHNIQUE: wool embroidery using chain stitch, flat stitch, French knots, and back stitch

SUPPLIES:

- wool yarn, Mora yarn, or equivalent, in various colors
- homespun, broadcloth, or other sturdy wool fabric, approximately 14 x 33 cm/ 5.5" x 12.9"
- 1 zipper, approximately 15 cm x 5.9"

PATTERN: see page 122

METHOD: Broadcloth and homespun don't fray, so generally speaking, you don't need to zigzag the edges. Draw the pattern using a marker pen. Embroider the wool embroidery using one or two threads wool yarn, depending on the thickness.

Stretch the embroidery according to instructions on page 91 and let dry. Take out the thumbtacks and cut away about 1 cm/ 0.4" around the edges, to get rid of the holes left by the tacks. Fold the embroidery face to face and sew the side and bottom edges together. Fold a thin hem at the top and sew the zipper by hand. If you like, you can sew on a sturdy ribbon for a handle.

TOTE BAG: BRITA-KAJSA RECYCLED

This tote bag is decorated with an authentic *Anundsjö* pattern, created by Brita-Kajsa herself. In order to add something of my own, I chose to sew the pattern by machine, rather than by hand. It's also faster that way. When embroidering by machine, it's a good idea to keep a support fabric underneath to avoid bunching. Just be sure to pin the two fabrics together properly.

TECHNIQUE: *Anundsjö* stitch
SUPPLIES:

- red sewing thread
- cotton fabric, 2 pieces of 32 x 41 cm/ 12.6" x 16.1" each, 2 pieces of 6 x 68 cm/ 26.8" each
- liner fabric, if you chose, 2 pieces of 32 x 38 cm/ 12.6" x 15" each
- a piece of sheeting (somewhat larger than the embroidery)

PATTERN: see page 123

METHOD: Zigzag all raw edges of fabric. Draw the patterns on one of the pieces of cotton fabric. Pin the sheeting onto the back. Make sure that it really covers the pattern you're going to embroider and that it's properly aligned. Sew straight stitch on the machine through all contours. If desired, fill certain shapes by sewing straight, turning, and sewing back right next to it. Repeat this step until the seams cover the shape. Thread all threads on the face of the fabric through to the back using a needle and fasten them on the back. Take out the pins and if you like, cut some of the supporting fabric off.

Assembling the tote: Place the pieces of liner fabric face to face and sew them together using the sewing machine, leaving a 1 cm/ 0.4" seam allowance on the long ends and on one short end. Press all seams apart using an iron. Do the same with the outer fabric. Turn so that the embroidery faces out. Fit the lining into the outer fabric (and leave it the way it is, so that you can see the pretty lining inside the tote). Fold the upper edge double and pin down. Put the bag aside while sewing the handles. Fold these pieces of fabric double lengthwise and press with an iron. Fold each half in and press again. Each handle should now be 1.5 cm/ 0.6" wide. Pin and sew a straight stitch along the long ends, as close to the edge as possible. Make a fold about 2 cm/ 0.8" from the edge at each end. Insert each fold under the hem of the bag and pin down. Make sure both handles end up even on both the front and back of the tote. Sew everything down with a seam 1.5 cm/ 0.6" from the edge of the bag. Reinforce with a small seam by each handle.

MITTENS: WINTER ROSEHIPS

I have to admit that it's a bit tricky to embroider finished gloves, but it's absolutely worth the effort. The result is jewel-like and it's not surprising that embroidered gloves were used at weddings, especially in Dalarna. This design is sewn from grey broadcloth, but you can embroider knit mittens too. Make sure that they're finely knit, or the embroidery won't look right.

TECHNIQUE: "sew-on"
SUPPLIES:

- wool yarn, Tuna wool yarn, or equivalent, in various colors
- a pair of mittens

PATTERN: see page 124

METHOD: Measure out the center of the mitten. Transfer the pattern using a marker pen so that it ends up on the center of the back of the hand. You may need to fill in the pattern as you go along. If it disappears you end up handling it quite a bit during the embroidery process. Keep one hand inside the mitt and try to keep the fabric as flat and even as possible. Use a light hand when you sew and don't tug too much at the floss. When you're done, turn the mitt inside out and secure all ends.

BOOK COVER: SKÅNE BIRD

I don't really know what to call this cover for a notebook. Folkloric perhaps? It's a mix of all manner of materials and colors. In any case, the motifs, which include a geometric star, are common in textiles from the south of Sweden.

TECHNIQUE: chain stitch and appliqué
SUPPLIES:

- cotton fabric
- broadcloth, or craft felt
- linen floss
- sewing thread
- lace
- sequins
- a notebook

PATTERN: see page 125

METHOD: Place the notebook on the fabric and mark a 1 cm/ 0.4" hem around the short edges and 8 cm/ 3.1" along each long edge. Cut and zigzag around the fabric. Fold the fabric double and mark where the front of the book is supposed to be. Draw the pattern using a marker pen, or a pencil. Embroider the star shape using chain stitch. Pin the lace so that it ends up in the center of the spine, and sew it down using small stitches. Cut out a bird, hearts, circles, or other shapes out of the craft felt and sew them on. Decorate further with embroidery and sequins. Iron the finished embroidery from the back.

Fold in the hem. It should be 1 cm/ 0.4" wide, and press it with an iron. Fold the fabric around the book and fold in the 8 cm/ 3.1"-wide hem. Sew it down at the bottom and at the top using small, close stitches on the front and back.

SUPPLIES

There aren't many limits when it comes to material used in embroidery. You can embroider on almost anything, using almost anything, as long as you have the right kind of needle. The most important thing is that the needle be big enough. The needle, not the floss, is what makes holes in the fabric. As long as you have the appropriate needle, you can sew using thick knitting yarn, ribbons, string, or thin sewing thread, on cotton, linen, velvet, or paper. Take a look at what you have at home before you start stocking up on (unfortunately rather expensive) specialty floss. This book is mainly intended to inspire you to create embroideries of your own, so feel free to try new things!

If you still want to follow the embroideries exactly as given here, these are the materials I've used:

FLOSS

DMC MOULINÉ: A mercerized cotton floss, this means that it's shinier than regular cotton. It can be found in most yarn, fabric, and craft stores and comes in a wide range of colors. You buy it in skeins and every thread consists of six thinner threads intertwined. You can use as many as you'd like to create a thicker, or thinner, embroidery. It is most common to use two or three threads at a time.

PEARL FLOSS: This too is mercerized cotton floss, more tightly wound than the mouliné. Pearl floss comes in various thicknesses and thus doesn't need to be split into threads.

DMC EMBROIDERY FLOSS OR LUNA FLOSS: A more matte cotton floss that can be split into two or three threads for embroidering. The floss has great coverage and is the best choice for Järvsö and Delsbo stitch. Unfortunately, it can be a bit hard to find in stores, though you can usually find it on the Internet.

KLIPPAN'S LINEN FLOSS: Comes in skeins intended for embroidery and in many different colors. Linen floss has somewhat different properties than cotton. It doesn't lie as well on the fabric and gives a more sprawling effect.

DMC TAPESTRY WOOL: A rather fluffy and soft wool floss. It can be split in half and works well for Skåne wool embroidery.

MORA YARN: A thinner, more tightly wound, but still soft wool yarn. It's a good idea to use a few threads together to get good coverage for a pattern.

TUNA WOOL YARN: A somewhat rougher wool yarn, named for the town of Tuna in Sweden. It's equivalent to the floss I've used for the "sew-on" in this book. Both Mora and Tuna yarn come in skeins, so you need to make your own balls of wool before you start to embroider.

WEFT: There are several types of wool that are originally meant for weaving, but which can also be used for embroideries. The only drawback is that you have to buy an entire roll, or skein. It can be worth it for basic colors like white and red.

FABRIC

COTTON: The fabric best suited to embroidery is sheeting. Cut pieces from old sheets, or buy yard goods. It comes in every color imaginable.

TRICOT: Usually made from cotton, but tricot can be mixed with more elastic elastane, or polyester thread, as in tights and underwear. Tricot is knit rather than woven. That's what makes it more elastic. It's a bit trickier to embroider, but 100 percent cotton is not too difficult to embroider on.

LINEN: This too comes in many thicknesses and colors. It's important to keep in mind if the embroidery is to be done by the number of threads; that is, if you need to be able to count the threads. For blackwork you need evenweave for the pattern to come out right. For the other, free techniques you can use any linen you like.

WOOL: Homespun, broadcloth, and woolen upholstery fabric is available in well-stocked fabric stores and craft stores. It usually comes in different colors.

TOOLS

The only things you really need for embroidering, apart from floss and fabric, are the following:

NEEDLES: As previously mentioned, these need to be adjusted according to the thickness of the floss. Tapestry needles in various sizes are best for embroidery. They have an oblong, somewhat flat eye with plenty of space for the floss. For wool embroidery you need a not overly thick darning needle. Sewing needles are used for hemming and sewing the projects, unless you do that by machine. Pins are a must for mounting.

EMBROIDERY HOOP: This tool makes most embroidery easier. It can be difficult to keep the fabric taught enough without a hoop, and it's easy to pull the floss too tight if you don't have one.

This is how to use a hoop: Place the fabric over one ring, making sure that the pattern you're about to embroider ends up in the middle. Stretch it into place using the other ring. Pull the fabric, equally in all directions, so that it's smooth. When you're finished embroidering the area that fit in the hoop, move it to the next spot. I tend to use a hoop for all types of patterns, except for long floral stems sewn using chain stitch, in which the stitches don't bunch much. With those you cover a lot of ground fast and constantly moving the hoop is a hassle.

SCISSORS: Embroidery scissors should be small, pointed, and sharp. Don't use them for anything else than fabric and floss, or they will quickly lose their edge.

PENS: A medium hard, newly sharpened, pencil works well for drawing patterns on light-colored fabrics. Use a light hand so that you don't end up with too much pencil on the fabric. Generally speaking, the lines come out in one wash and the idea is for the floss to cover the pencil lines, but if you draw too hard they might show through.

For darker fabrics you need a white or light-colored marker pen. You can buy one in a well-stocked fabric store. There are also special pens where the lines disappear with water, or from exposure to air after a while, but they're rather hard to find.

TRANSFERRING PATTERNS

Feel free to use the patterns at the back of the book for your embroideries, either in whole, or parts of them. Put the tracing paper (supplied on the inside back cover of this book), or any other thin sketch paper, over them and trace. If a pattern feels wrong size-wise for what you want to embroider, you can adjust it first, using a copy machine. Put the book in and either enlarge, or scale down the pattern as needed. I recommend that you draw each stitch on the paper. This will help you understand how to fill the pattern in with floss on fabric. It doesn't need to be exact, but it will give you an idea of how to embroider. Also look at photographs and drawings of how the stitches are laid.

There are a few different methods for transferring patterns to fabric. If you feel confident, you can draw freehand and adjust the pattern according to the fabric you want to embroider. If the fabric is light in color and not too thick, you can put the drawing under it and fill in the lines using a pen. It also helps to hold the drawing and fabric up to a window, or to put it all on a light table.

For darker and thicker fabrics, you can make little holes in the tracing paper using a thick needle along all lines. Next, draw over the holes using a white marker pen. The pattern will show up as little dots on the fabric.

Templates are usually used for "sew-on," *Järvsö* stitch, and *Delsbo* stitch. Copy the pattern in the book, first on tracing paper, then on thicker cardboard. Cut out shapes, place on the fabric, and trace along the edges.

For *Halland* stitch, which is based on round shapes, you can use whatever round objects you have at home: gasses, mugs, tea candles, etc.

TECHNIQUE AND CARE

Once you've drawn the pattern on the fabric, stretched it on the hoop, and chosen floss, it's finally time to start to embroider! Never begin by tying a knot on the floss. Instead, insert the needle a bit further down, bring it through on the line you're starting on,

and secure the thread later. Knots can come undone and if they do, you'll have a little tuft of floss sticking up in the middle of your embroidery. Not fun. However, once you're underway and are about to change floss, you can secure it under the existing stitches. That way you'll save floss and avoid lots of loose ends hanging out of the embroidery. Securing threads are among the most boring things out there, so it's nice to get it done while you're embroidering.

It's a good idea to sew from right to left as much as possible. That way you will avoid the floss coming unraveled and lessen the risk of knots. Also, don't embroider using threads that are too long. That will also increase the risk of knots.

Other than that, the most important thing is to remember not to pull too hard. Make a stitch and pull the floss through until the fabric tells you to stop. Place the floss roughly the way you drew the pattern and always follow the lines. Use a light hand and try to maintain a good tempo. Don't fuss too much with each stitch; if you do it's easy to get discouraged.

AFTERCARE: With most projects in this book it is enough to simply iron the fabric when you're done. Press from behind, preferably with a moist cloth between the iron and the fabric.

Wool embroidery contracts in a way that can't be ironed out. You need to stretch that type of embroidery in order to make it smooth. This is how to do it: Attach the finished embroidery to a piece of wood that isn't too hard, using thumbtacks. Make sure the fabric is aligned and stretched equally in each direction. Place the thumbtacks densely along the outer edge. Place a moist cloth over it and let it sit until the cloth has dried. Linen and cotton fabric can be stretched on an ironing board using pins. This method will ensure the fabric is smooth without the finished embroidery ending up too flat, which can easily happen when you press with an iron.

WASHING: It's a good idea to wash the fabric before you begin embroidering. That way you can be sure it won't shrink later and ruin your work. Most embroideries in this book can be washed by hand, or by machine on a cold cycle. If you want to machine wash wool embroideries you need to select the wool cycle. It's as gentle as washing by hand. For best results, use a detergent made for wool or delicates.

EMBROIDERY LESSON

RUNNING STITCH: Pass the needle up through the fabric and then down again a bit further away.

BACK STITCH: Bring the needle up through the fabric and then take a small backward stitch. Continue so that the next stitch begins where the last one ended.

WHIPPED RUNNING STITCH: Sew a line of running stitch. On your way back, thread the needle through the stitch, instead of the fabric.

CROSS STITCH: Sew diagonal stitches over a number of threads in the fabric. Turn and sew your way back in the other direction. Cross stitch is easiest to do on evenweave linen, or Aida.

STEM STITCH: This is sewn like back stitch, only you bring the needle through next to the previous stitch. Make sure the floss always ends up on the same side of the needle when you make a new stitch.

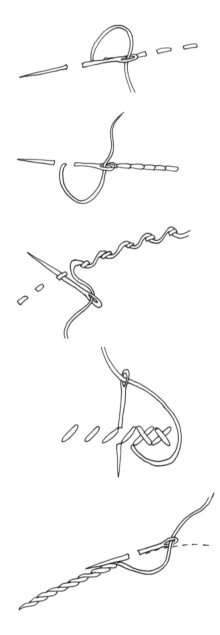

CHAIN STITCH: Bring the needle through the fabric and down again, right next to where you brought it up. Bring the needle through again a bit further down. Loop the floss around the needle, stretch the floss a bit, and bring the needle through the fabric. If you instead bring the needle down a little ways away from where you first brought it through, you'll have open chain stitch. Chain stitch can also be used to cover larger surfaces by simply sewing several rows of stitches close to one another.

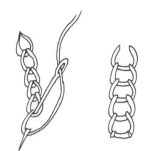

Chain stitch, regular and open

You can sew flowers too.

ONE-SIDED FLAT STITCH: Bring the needle through on the line you've drawn. Pull it down on the other side of the shape you're embroidering and immediately make a tiny stitch to the side. The floss will now be visible mainly on the face of the fabric.

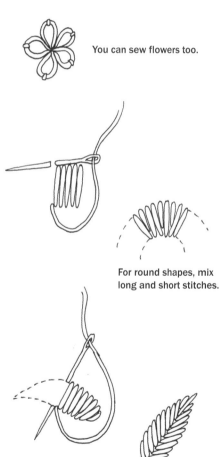

For round shapes, mix long and short stitches.

SATIN STITCH: Sew even stitches over the shape you've drawn. Bring the needle through and up again, right next to the previous stitch. You will now have thread on both the face and the back of the fabric. This gives a rounder shape than the one-sided flat stitch.

Leaves can also be sewn this way.

FRENCH KNOTS: Wind the floss, where it comes up through the fabric, two or more turns around the needle and bring it down through right next to where you brought it up. Carefully pull the needle through. It's a good idea to resist a bit with your thumb so that you don't lose tension in the floss.

ENCROACHING SATIN STITCH: Sew one-sided flat stitch, or satin stitch, vertically against the line you've drawn. Make stitches a suitable length. Continue with a row under, either using the same floss, or a different color. This technique is perfect for covering large areas, or creating interesting color variations.

COUCHING: Lay a thread along the line you're sewing. Attach it to the fabric by sewing tiny, even, stitches over the entire thread.

BUTTONHOLE STITCH: Bring the needle through on the line you've drawn. Bring it down a bit further away and down again on the first line. Place the floss around the needle and bring it through. If you sew this stitch in a round circle you end up with a wheel. Sew the stitch inward, or outward, according to the effect you want to create.

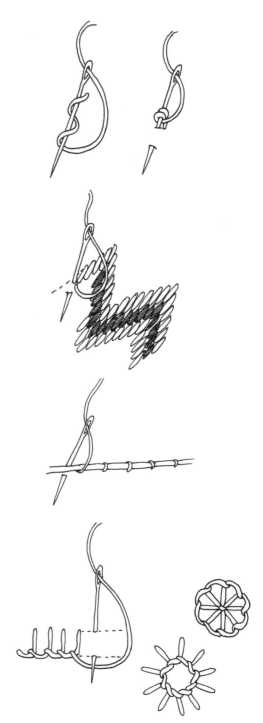

94

HERRINGBONE STITCH: Sew a rather long, diagonal stitch to the left. Make a small stitch in the fabric toward you and then make another long stitch, to the right this time. If you leave some space between stitches you get a herringbone stitch. If you make the next stitch right next to the first, you get a denser effect.

TASSEL STITCH: Bring the needle through by the number one on the illustration. Bring it down by the two, through by the three, and so on. Make sure that the one and the eight end up close to each other so that the tassel ends up nice and dense.

ANUNDSJÖ STITCH: Sew a one-sided flat stitch, but bring the needle through in the middle of the stitch you just made and attach one thread with a small stitch to the side. This diagonal stitch can be made either to the left or to the right. For Anundsjö stitch you need a floss that can easily be split, that is to say: at least two threads that aren't wound too tight.

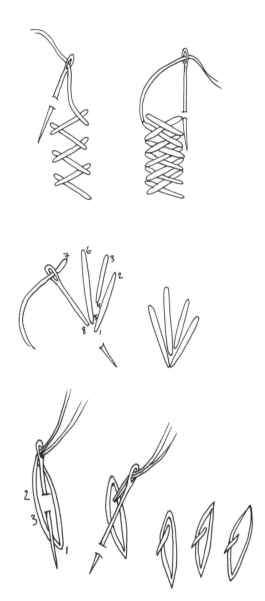

LAID FILLING STITCH: This stitch can be varied infinitely. Start by drawing a shape—a circle is the most common. Then stretch floss, either along the thread, or diagonal, to form a net. Attach the net to the fabric using various types of stitches (see illustration). Try mixing different colors for further effect. Finish with a border of chain stitch, back stitch, stem stitch, or the like, to cover the edge. A hoop is an absolute must for this technique! You can also make it a bit easier on yourself by drawing the net, ever so faintly, using a pencil or marker pen.

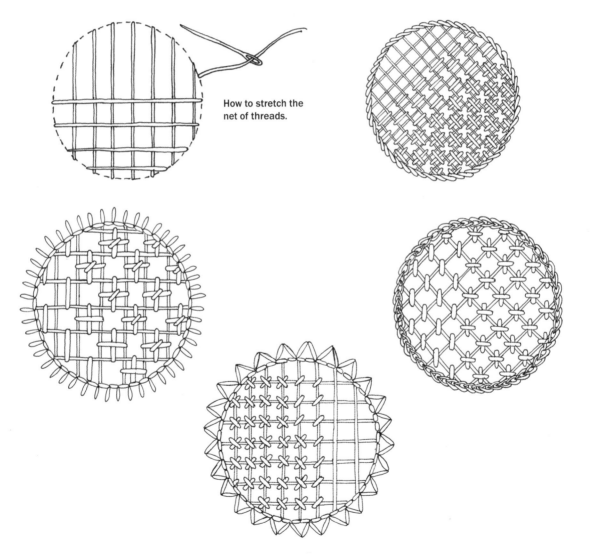

How to stretch the net of threads.

HEMSTITCH: Carefully cut three threads in the fabric, parallel to the hem and right underneath it. Pull the threads out. Attach a few stitches in the fabric, wind the thread once or twice around three threads in the fabric, and then make a new stitch. Continue all the way. The threads in the fabric will contract and form little holes. Do the same on the other edge.

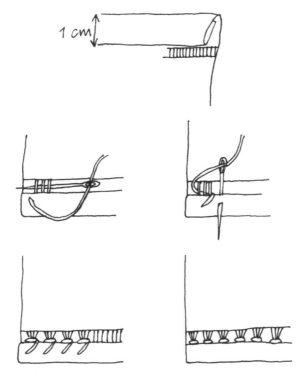

Back   Face

PATTERNS

Enlarge or scale down patterns as needed, using a copy machine before transferring them to the fabric.

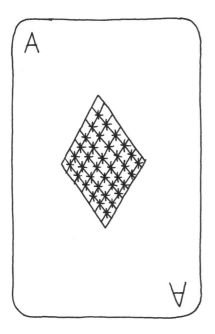

100

106

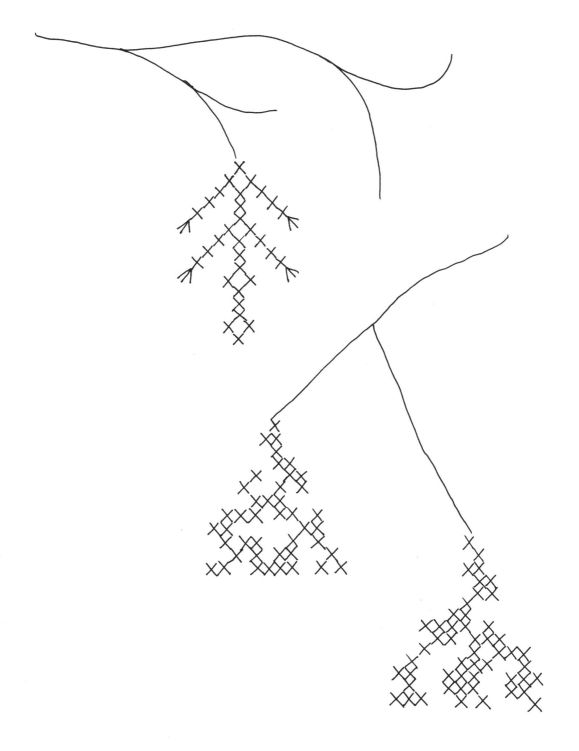

110

115

117

you can have it all

123

ACKNOWLEDGMENTS

Eva Kruk: Editor extraordinaire! Your ability to structure everything, combined with your confidence in me and interest in embroidery has been incredibly rewarding. I couldn't have asked for a better supervisor.

Karin Björkquist: Thank you for a smooth and fun collaboration. Your opinions and ideas on how to make the photos gave a whole new (and better) life to the embroideries. You also made sure we had a steady supply of coffee and cake!

Victoria Kapadia Bergmark: So much more than a designer! You had us all in a good mood and offered everything: from homemade marmalade to inspiring conversation and lots of good laughs. I've had full confidence in you throughout this project.

Mom, Dad, and Mats: My fan club!

Thanks to my teachers and mentors at HV, who were with me during the beginning of what would later become this book. A special thanks to Carita Landstedt, Gun Aschan, and Kim Halle: I will always carry your advice with me.

All the models who happily participated: Mats Holmberg, Emilia Öster, Susanne El Makdisi, Victoria Kapadia Bergmark, Iris Kapadia Bergmark, Louise Björkquist, Owen Hardwicke, Johan Sellén, and Malin Nilsson—I'm so glad you wanted to be in on this!

Finally, I'd like to thank the great friends who one way or another have been engaged or involved in the creation of this book: Sarah, Alex, Anna O., Anna S., Kenza, Helén, Bojana, Heléne, Magda, Ottil, Rebecca, Niklas H., Niklas M., Jonas, Erika, Jenny, Gunilla, Mia, Audrey and Frida who've blogged, all the Irises, and all my other friends, acquaintances, and relatives who've given encouragement while I've been embroidering. It's meant so much.

An extra warm thank you also goes to Mattias, who wanted a hoodie of his very own.

BIBLIOGRAPHY

Bergström-Granquist, Emy. *Svenska mönsterboken del XIV: Svartstick från Leksands socken, Dalarna*. Stockholm, 1942.

Brodén, Märta. *Delsbosöm: långsöm och tofssöm från Delsbo*. LTs förlag, 1979.

Dandanell, Birgitta (ed). *Påsöm: folkligt broderi från Floda i Dalarna*. Dalarnas museum, 1992.

Eldvik, Berit och Åsbrink, Brita. *Järvsösöm*. LTs förlag, 1979.

Hådell, Anna. *Svartstick*. LTs förlag, 1979.

Johansson, Britta. *Hallandsöm*. LTs förlag, 1977.

Kristiansson, Maj-Britt. *Anundsjösöm*. LTs förlag, 1978.

The collections at Nordiska Muséet.

INDEX